VIBRANT INTERIORS

VIBRANT INTERIORS
LIVING LARGE AT HOME

ANDREA MONATH SCHUMACHER

GIBBS SMITH
TO ENRICH AND INSPIRE HUMANKIND

To Calvin Thomas Schumacher and
Charlisse Elizabeth Monath Schumacher:
you're my heart and soul.

INTRODUCTION

This book is a glimpse into my world as a designer and a small vignette of my personal experience with amazing humans that make up the world of design. I'd like to think my talent and creativity are backed by my education, but my true knowledge of design comes from a long and ongoing love of the world around me. While I was growing up, my father's career in virology took our family to live everywhere from Nigeria to Boston, not to mention our trips around the globe.

Each country we visited opened my eyes to the vibrancy of the world. Now, as an adult with wanderlust, I travel for inspiration and to get a fresh perspective on interiors. My consistent takeaway is that the magic is in the mix of antiques, showstopping art, and lighting. Juxtaposing these elements with clean-lined upholstered goods achieves just the right balance.

My grandmother, the artist Elizabeth Monath—who was an understudy of Fernand Léger and Salvador Dalí in the 1930s in Paris—taught me the art of living. I spent my childhood summers with her in her art studio, learning to draw and picking botanicals and pressing them with ink, all the while soaking up her fearlessness and boundless energy.

Now I live and breathe design, and I pinch myself daily in gratitude that my career has given me the opportunity to touch people's lives. At ASI, we not only create each space for living large in a vibrant way but also enhance it in ways you may not notice, like how something functions or subtle design elements that reveal themselves over time. I am a firm believer that great design lies in the details.

city STYLE

Every New York City expat knows the elation that comes from finally having a home with boundless space after years of feeling hemmed in. So, when a family of fresh Manhattan transplants moved into this 1909 Tudor Revival, we upped the airy, spacious vibe while bringing in exquisite elements of urban life, like an irresistible cocktail bar.

It helped that these clients already owned the best-possible muse to set the tone. Their art collection is museum-worthy, ranging from a nineteenth-century portrait of George Washington attributed to Rembrandt Peale to graphic works by abstract photorealist painter Jeanette Pasin Sloan. Each piece kicked off the palette of saturated hues and calm blue-grays, bringing a heady splash of color to the space.

Taking pride of place in their entry hall: a circa 1760 walnut French provincial console the homeowners found in the Paris flea market. As a foil—and to prevent the room from reading overly historic—we hung a modern wallcovering that's cerebral and inviting and adds a necessary dose of play. Use your foyer to make a great first impression, like a firm handshake.

PREVIOUS OVERLEAF: Placing furniture and fixtures symmetrically in the foyer creates a sense of calm and peace. OPPOSITE: Once a formal dining room, this space now acts as a family room, with a built-in cabinet for storage and a multiuse ottoman.

Design recipe: mix genres, eras, textures, and price points. Then stir.

We turned the former dining area into a de facto family room, with a small TV and plenty of lounging spots. The pinstripe chairs all swivel, so if someone's cooking in the adjacent kitchen, you can whirl around and chat with them comfortably. Overhead, classic pendant fixtures echo the coffered ceiling and the iron drapery rods.

Throughout the home, conversation pieces reign. I firmly believe that a house should never be too serious—you always need to dot a room with pieces that are kind of hilarious, almost so ridiculous and whimsical that they spark a dialogue. For example, in the main living room, you'll see a midcentury brass slipper chair with legs that look like snakes. On the blue silk draperies, a leading-edge trim brings in the clouds from the entry for an underlying theme that's not in-your-face. We also had the Lucite cocktail table lacquered a powdery cerulean blue. That's something

PREVIOUS OVERLEAF, LEFT: Draperies that appear hand-painted supply an artful feel.
PREVIOUS OVERLEAF, RIGHT: Hammered-iron stools are upholstered in a nubby ombré silk. OPPOSITE: Graphic pieces by Jeanette Pasin Sloan grace the intricately carved original mantel. OVERLEAF: Occasional chairs in unusual shapes act as conversation starters.

Live in your home like a star, surrounded in luxury.

to keep in mind as you're revamping a home—these days, anything can be redone in a different color.

Prior to starting this project, the corner of the living room where the bar now stands consisted of a little-used piano on a step-up landing. To make it more luscious than lackluster, we built an island where a wine fridge and ice maker are hidden so that when you're in the living room, you see only the beautiful cabinetry and quartzite, but when you're behind the bar mixing drinks, everything utilitarian is within easy reach. (Speaking of secrets, the art piece on the left side of the bar is actually a television for when you feel like bellying up and watching a game.) Behind it all, we installed an antiqued mirror wall to bounce light back into the room. It's almost like another window and casts the whole space in as much palpable glamour as any Upper East Side *boîte*. Cheers to that.

Gold-framed artworks, including a 19th-century portrait of George Washington that presides over the bar, are all the more magnetic when hung against textural, gray-blue grass cloth walls.

OPPOSITE: This snake occasional chair is a midcentury modern original. ABOVE, CLOCKWISE FROM TOP LEFT: Plaster lamps on scalloped tables echo the plaster sconces in this home's entrance. Blue silk draperies with a leading-edge trim nod to the foyer's cloud wallcovering. In Chinese culture, the dragon represents good luck, strength, and health. A prideful peacock dominates a throw pillow.

The ceiling is often called the "fifth wall." Wallpapering the ceiling—either with a textural paper or graphic pattern—draws the eye upward and envelops the room.

Make a maximalist statement by enveloping a room in one fabulous pattern, like this latticed chocolate and cream motif. The palm-leaf chandelier plays off the bamboo lattice wallcovering.

PREVIOUS OVERLEAF: In an otherwise traditional kitchen, a trio of oversized octagonal pendant light fixtures over the island make a statement. ABOVE: The zebra rugs give a grounding graphic pattern to the room. OPPOSITE: The multipurpose dining room is lined with books and board games for daily use, with the option to be formal on special occasions.

PREVIOUS OVERLEAF, LEFT: Ornate windowpanes demand equally ornate—but modern—draperies. PREVIOUS OVERLEAF, RIGHT: Mimicking the juxtaposition on the opposite wall, artist Bob Knox deconstructs an old *House Beautiful* magazine image. ABOVE: A pristine white linen chaise is ready for curling up in anytime. The sculptural mirror reflects light back into the room. OPPOSITE: In the primary bedroom, we emphasized the four-post bed's artful lines by selecting a textural off-white grass cloth backdrop.

ABOVE: In a classic powder bath with floor-to-ceiling antique mirrored tile, a sculptural sconce adds wow factor. OPPOSITE: There's nothing like a classic soaking tub—especially one bathed in natural light. OVERLEAF: Abundant embroidery and carved wood antiques are a favorite way to add texture.

conversation STARTERS

It sounds crazy, but it's true: If you think back on some of the best conversations you've ever had—those moments when you truly connected with another person, soul to soul—chances are you were comfortably seated. I try to build what I call "conversation starters" in every single project I do: a collection of four lounge chairs set around a tea-height table.

I often custom-make the latter at 24 inches tall. It's a superb height for chitchat, playing board games, or even eating a meal, because it's tall enough to get your knees under. A formal dining table just doesn't compare, at least when it comes to the laid-back lounge factor.

In each conversation starter room, I'm also careful to decorate the space with pieces that could serve to kick-start a conversation with a stranger. Old friends can get past small talk fast, but new acquaintances sometimes need a little jump—anything that's not vanilla. Maybe it's wallpaper festooned with illustrations of Great Danes or your dog breed of choice. Or a quirky piece of art you lugged home from Europe on that backpacking trip in college.

I never forget to finish each space with mood lighting in the form of a twinkling chandelier to cast a romantic glow (so everyone looks their best), bolster pillows for back support, and something soft underfoot—all there to encourage conversations to linger as long as possible.

ABOVE: At a round table, everyone is on equal footing. In this San Francisco home, a built-in banquette gives the homeowner a myriad of seating options. OPPOSITE: The tile floor welcomes a faux fur rug you can sink your toes into.

great ESCAPE

Ｗhat if every single day of your life felt like a vacation? Dream scenario, right? That's what these longtime clients had in mind for their family's new 12,000-square-foot modern Montauk-style home. They enlisted me to give it the effortlessly luxe feeling of a seafront resort inspired by their frequent sojourns in the Hamptons.

Now, bringing beach vibes to a landlocked state isn't exactly easy, so I began by setting a neutral tone with black and white finishes that will never go out of style. Graphic and strong, the ineffably chic color pairing has the wow factor of a tuxedo. And it's more than just timeless: it forms a placid backdrop for a scant dusting of color—like smoky blues, seaweed greens, and scarlet sunset reds you'll see here—that lets the more vibrant hue take center stage.

For the warmest possible welcome, we created an enveloping black entrance hall with marble checkerboard floors and textural black grass cloth walls. This diminutive vestibule was inspired by Frank Lloyd Wright, who always gave homes a cramped foyer so people would have a feeling of delighted surprise when they stepped foot in the actual living spaces. Here, the living room ceiling soars more than twelve

PREVIOUS OVERLEAF: A marble checkerboard tile floor is a classic entry choice that summons classic Montauk. OPPOSITE: Sometimes, placing books backward on a shelf—so their spines face the wall—allows other art and *objets* to shine.

feet, so we brought it down to earth a bit by arranging the layout symmetrically for a calming, restful effect. I also kept the homeowner's existing twin sofas from their last home and had them recovered. (I try not to scrap everything—we owe it to the earth.)

To give the adjacent dining area the aura of a jubilant night on the town, we designed it to look like a restaurant's private dining space, complete with its own glass-enclosed wine room. Earthy materials always add instant tranquility, so when I spotted a live-edge slab of black walnut tree at a furniture warehouse in L.A., I immediately contacted my client and we had it shipped in for the custom dining table. Paired with bespoke chairs upholstered in a faux bois cut velvet for plush texture, it lugs the beachiness of driftwood into the otherwise sleek space, and helps put guests at ease.

Because my client is up at dawn for his job, the office was purposefully placed at the opposite end of the home from the bedrooms to ensure privacy. No one who works this hard should be without a power desk, so for this client—the first to ever hire me for a

By placing the client's pair of newly reupholstered, light-bronze velvet sofas symmetrically aligned with the built-in bookshelves, it effectively puts the spotlight on the modern painting and playful light fixture.

The homeowners' own collection of carnival glass vases. This handmade iridescent glassware was highly coveted in the roaring 1920s, and lends a vintage appeal to the room.

ABOVE, CLOCKWISE FROM TOP LEFT: Custom faux bois cut velvet dining chairs. A chandelier with all the effervescence of champagne bubbles. A huge slab of black walnut makes for an artful dining table. Even table bases should be eye-catching. OPPOSITE: The open bar imparts a festive feeling.

An office doesn't just mean business; it can also be a sanctuary. Make it vibrant.

residential project, who believed in me from the start and helped launch my career—we built a seven-foot-long bureau. We stained it my favorite emerald green of all time (Cat's Eye by Benjamin Moore, which almost looks like malachite and is extra energizing) and paired it with 1970s wood-frame barrel chairs that we upholstered for cushy, lasting comfort.

But arguably the space with the most carefree vacay feel is the open kitchen and family room, where exposed rafters in a salty gray echo the airiness of a dockside lobster shack. Sandy-hued custom sectionals await sprawled-out family time, and outside the wall of French doors, a turquoise pool and tennis courts beckon. It may come as no surprise that these clients didn't want a TV in here—all the better to connect and unplug together. The result, even on gray and drizzly days, is pure Montauk in August.

For a sun-drenched room we painted the paneling black to absorb light. Bonus: the dark wall color camouflages built-in speakers.

OPPOSITE: In this client's office, walls painted in Benjamin Moore Black Beauty hide a jib door—a secret portal to a hallway and powder room. ABOVE: Paneled walls give this otherwise modernist bathroom an aura of history. OVERLEAF: Twin sectionals give the whole family plenty of room to lounge.

Lively objects that reflect and ricochet light around the room create vibrancy, which elevates your living space. Find ways to capture the sun using found objects, large or small.

ABOVE: A granite backsplash is as beguiling as an art piece behind the range.
OPPOSITE: This glass-enclosed wine room was meant to mimic one at a renowned restaurant that's a favorite of the family.

The built environment directly affects your emotions. Design your home to make you feel wonderful and in shades that are complementary to you. For example, if you have blue eyes, accentuate that with your finish choices.

OPPOSITE: Mixing blue-and-white patterns comes easily in the breakfast nook, where the refreshing color combo makes a prime way to start the day. OVERLEAF: Hand-painted and embroidered silk wallcoverings in the primary bedroom have the wow effect of a coveted art piece.

PREVIOUS OVERLEAF, LEFT AND RIGHT: The only thing better than tufting? Pink tufting. Koi drawer pulls on the bedside tables reflect the custom wallcoverings. ABOVE: Hanging a pendant light before a mirror doubles its glow. OPPOSITE: The metallic-finish soaking tub shimmers at night under the light of a Swarovski crystal chandelier.

ABOVE: Gleaming black and white subway tiles paired with brass fixtures give this bath the storied effect of a 1920s original. OPPOSITE: We painted the homeowners' formerly black canopy bed a crisp white to shed a spotlight on the room's cozy fireplace.

living COLOR

I'll do anything for my clients, but when they ask me not to use color, it's a challenge (even though I still take it on with gusto). To me, vibrant interiors are part of what helps your home tell your story and are key to a life well lived.

If you're new to decorating with all the spectrums of color, I know it can be intimidating. I often start by choosing one multicolored element in a room to be the impetus for the palette—whether it's a client's prized painting or a piece of pottery inherited from their beloved uncle—and draw hues from it to outfit the rest of the space. Even a piece of fabric can make a perfect jumping-off point.

There's also no shame in starting small with color. Sometimes, dipping your toe in is better than wallpapering an entire room in a tint you'll regret. Buy a sculptural lamp in a radiant hue that catches your eye. Or unfurl a graphic and spirited area rug, always a wonderful way to ground a space and one you can easily stow away if it doesn't make you happy any longer.

Not sure what hues to choose, when the human eye can distinguish around a million of them? Proceed directly to your closet or armoire for inspiration. The wardrobe within is often a great reflection of your tastes, not to mention what you look good in. If you love it, you can't go wrong.

ABOVE: Ringing the dining table with plush armchairs gives guest and host alike top-tier seating.
OPPOSITE: We pulled this dining room's enveloping deep emerald-green wall color from the art piece then selected every other element in the room to complement it, down to the ethereal ghost chairs.

rustic
REVAMP

Y ou don't have to be a Hollywood director to create a cinematic scene. All you need is a beguiling setting and a cast of head-turning characters. Unfortunately, when we first walked into the house on this legendary 4,000-acre Wyoming ranch (the former home of Mary O'Hara, author of the 1941 novel *My Friend Flicka*), the interiors were what La La Land producers would affectionately call a flop. There were linoleum floors and tiled counters in the kitchen, gloomy and dark spaces, carpeted bathrooms . . . the list goes on!

But when it came to riveting characters, Remount Ranch had unforgettable ones that formed the backbone of our revamp. Take the bar, built circa 1946 when the place was a dude ranch. We kept it pristine, down to the antique pistol wallpaper and brass footrail burnished by cowboy boots over the decades. Proof it's as authentic as it gets? A horsehair halter made by Tom Horn, an outlaw Steve McQueen played in the 1980 Western *Tom Horn*, presides over the place.

The ranch's original 1886 homestead remained, too, complete with its log and chinking walls and kiva fireplaces. Over time, it had become the main dining room. We kept my client's own burl-leg table and hickory stick-wood side chairs but added global touches like a late-nineteenth-century Chinese buffet and a Yoruba-beaded headdress from Nigeria. On the back of new library chairs we installed for a cozier

PREVIOUS OVERLEAF: We found a pair of antique ram candle sconces and had them electrified. OPPOSITE: For the entrance hall of this storied Wyoming ranch, we took a regular shed-antler chandelier and had it coated in a fire engine red high-gloss lacquer.

Approach interiors with an open mind, drawing inspiration from other cultures and fashion.

feel, a chinoiserie toile, glazed-linen fabric pioneered the entire color palette for the whole project. It has a saturated, mystical feel that speaks to the homeowners' spirituality and can stand up to the jaw-dropping landscape beyond the windows.

Nobody in Wyoming, the least-populated state in the nation, should ever feel cramped. So, in the adjacent family room, we expanded the footprint by ten feet so the homeowners' frequent houseguests—including grown kids and grandkids— would have plenty of room to roam. Wood-block forest wallcovering I designed using my grandmother Elizabeth Burger Monath's own artwork makes the space feel as boundless as the ranch's acreage, while plaid draperies and chandeliers hung by equestrian stirrups are like a Ralph Lauren fever dream sprung to life. Where previous owners turned the exterior walls of the original cabin into a courtyard, we created a billiard room with wallpaper I had custom-printed from a 1960s newspaper article about the ranch by the *Laramie Boomerang*.

PREVIOUS OVERLEAF: Woodsy wallpaper based on my grandmother's artwork—now available in my Liesl Collection of wallcoverings, textiles, and trimmings—plays well with plaid draperies and pheasant-dotted velvet swivel chairs in the client's great room, with all the welcoming warmth of a ski lodge. OPPOSITE: We repeated the ranch's Double R monogram throughout the home for a thoroughly bespoke feeling.

FERNAND LÉGER

PREVIOUS OVERLEAF: The exposed-beam ceilings are original. CLOCKWISE FROM TOP LEFT: The home's circa 1800s stucco fireplace. Layering is crucial to make a place feel like it has stood the test of time. A pair of decorative hookahs act as sculptures. The homeowner's collection of cowboy hats, now a functional art installation. Custom refrigerator pulls inspired by the ranch's herd of longhorn cattle. The client's own burl-leg table.

Infuse your home with modern and vintage pieces. Storytelling happens when old collides with new.

A personal feel is always a must. Even in the parts of the property we took down to the studs, we used naturally aged, reclaimed barnwood as a finish to imbue rooms with the heady aura of Wild West history. When you're lucky enough to work on a storied property, you have to go big, pulling out the best elements of the backstory to propel the design forward. Here, we subtly repeated the double R monogram for Remount Ranch throughout the home, everywhere from the banquette in the billiard room to the railing in the upstairs kids' room. We even transformed the homeowner's massive collection of cowboy hats into an art installation by hanging them on custom hoof hooks made in Wyoming. We purposefully limited the number of seats in his book-lined private study so it could be his retreat, the proverbial man cave.

I've noticed over the years that when clients hired a separate kitchen designer, it made it difficult for the cook space to flow with the rest of the house. So, we do our

PREVIOUS OVERLEAF: A hand-hammered brass range hood glimmers in the kitchen.
OPPOSITE: Turquoise walls aren't what you might expect from a centuries-old Wyoming ranch, which was exactly why they were the perfect choice for this central hallway.

Nothing feels quite as cozy underfoot as deep sheepskin—a cloud-like choice for this seating area built for two, just steps from the wine fridge.

90

ABOVE: We preserved the ranch's hammered-copper bar almost exactly as it was, adding a Buddha for good luck. OPPOSITE: The gunslinging wallpaper sheathing the timeworn bar is original.

The Cavalry Bar at Remount Ranch

PREVIOUS OVERLEAF: Note the original chinking and log walls from the ranch's early frontier cabin days. ABOVE: We had a 1960s newspaper article about the ranch made into custom wallpaper for the billiard room, which becomes a buzzing, after-hours hangout spot. OPPOSITE: The ranch's monogram is repeated in the nailhead design at the base of the custom, channeled, upholstered banquette.

ABOVE: We turned an antique dresser from Asia into the sink vanity in this powder room. The sconces are made of horsehair—a spirited touch under the barnwood ceiling. OPPOSITE: We opted for this crane wallcovering because it's symbolic of happiness and eternal youth.

OPPOSITE: We installed as many built-in bookshelves as possible in the homeowner's private study to house his collection of history books. The overscaled light fixture is masculine and dramatic. ABOVE: Snakeskin wallcovering adds a rebellious touch to this powder bath.

Every home needs a bar center stage. Why limit happy to one hour?

own in-house kitchen design and always integrate the aesthetic with the property at large. To add a dash of glam to this cook space, glossy wallpaper shines between beams of reclaimed barnwood on the low ceiling, bouncing light around like a mirror. The range hood was hand-hammered by our metalsmith; over the island, a lone glass ball in the light fixture glows at night, twisting in the air like a mobile. Thick quartzite counters culled from deep in the earth echo Wyoming's artful sandstone and shale rock outcroppings.

There are plenty of nods to nature throughout the ranch that stop short of being theme-y, including bronze refrigerator pulls in the shape of gazelle horns and an antler chandelier we opted to have custom painted a glossy red. How could there not be? It's all in testament to the wildness that flourishes here and can't be pinned down, from their own herd of Texas Longhorns to the antelope, bobcats, and mountain lions that occasionally wander the grounds, as if on cue.

PREVIOUS OVERLEAF: In the primary bedroom, an olive-green leather, metallic, and wood bed gives off an industrial feel. Grass cloth walls serve to visually soften the rough-hewn overhead beams. OPPOSITE: Every ranch demands at least one throwback Western movie poster; this one is from the third book of previous owner Mary O'Hara's *My Friend Flicka* series.

A hand-embroidered blanket I discovered in a Paris flea market provides enduring appeal in this guest room. OVERLEAF LEFT: Pull the Asian handles on this cabinet and you'll find a hot fuchsia interior. OVERLEAF RIGHT: In an ideal world, every guest room would be equipped with a seating area so guests can sip their morning coffee in peace.

ABOVE: A light fixture reminiscent of wisteria glimmers over the soaking tub in the primary bath. OPPOSITE: We tucked a custom glass door in this steam shower behind an antique Rajasthani archway; it feels like a threshold to another realm. OVERLEAF LEFT: These mermaid handles are one of my trademarks. OVERLEAF RIGHT: A blown-glass fixture above the bed casts a theatrical light over this guest room. PAGES 114–15: Kids and grandkids can roam wild on this antelope carpet.

SIGNATURE

tip the SCALE

It sounds counterintuitive, but when you juxtapose two different pieces of varying scales right next to one another, you can make each one look its best. Jewelry is a great example of this approach: When you place a colossal diamond on a whisper-thin gold band, each one sings a little more beautifully than it would if the stone were set on a clunky, equally blinged-out ring. Part of the appeal is in the marriage of two contrasts.

When a home's architecture is particularly lofty, with soaring ceilings, I try to think like a museum curator, sourcing furniture and pieces that complement the space. Go too far and it's garish. Stay too safe and a room doesn't feel "done." If there's a truly postcard-ready view out your windows, it's okay to allow that to be the star, keeping the rooms within the home to a more muted color palette that's taken from the sky and emerald evergreen trees beyond the glass. If you keep it earthy and organic, the eye is drawn outside, where it often belongs if you're in a vacationland.

Occasionally, it's less about a piece's actual scale than its shape and finish. Curvaceous, tufted footstools can look dynamite when paired against a cool, straight-edged floor. Ditto for a smooth, round stone sculpture placed alongside a time-worn wood table—all the better together.

ABOVE: We placed two cast root console tables end to end to fill an expansive wall in this living space and hung a mammoth horse painting above them. A duo of elegant starburst lamps have the delicate grace of raindrops. OPPOSITE: A cowhide adds softness underfoot in this towering living space.

calming
CAPE

Sometimes there's nothing more restorative than a stay along the sea. So, when my longtime client, who was raised on Cape Cod, wanted to downsize from a 12,000-square-foot property and build a lakefront house, we decided to summon the gracious feeling of a waterside resort with all the trimmings.

She enlisted a resort architect to design the property with high ceilings typical of a chalet. We also maximized the relaxing effect of the water by installing glass doors and clerestory windows to capture the glimmering lake, and creating a major architectural focal point in a cantilevered gas fireplace that sits open to the expansive great room's living and dining spaces on all sides. I sheathed its hood in a graphic wallpaper, pulling heady colors from it to form the great room's color palette, including the deep cornflower blue for the stain on the built-in bar.

Throughout, reflections of nature reign. On the painting in the foyer, tiny sailboats appear to bob on an ocean that echoes a rich sky above. Icicle-inspired lighting fixtures cast their magnetic glow over the fireside dining table. My client's

PREVIOUS OVERLEAF: An urchin chandelier, made of hand-cut leather in South Africa, appears to float over the foyer. OPPOSITE: We borrowed the cut lattice from the drawers in this centuries-old Chinese chest and repeated it in the stairway railing (behind the earthenware pots at right).

PREVIOUS OVERLEAF: In the great room, sliding glass doors stack to give the space an indoor-outdoor feel. The cantilevered gas fireplace is open on all sides, giving it the same vibe as one you'd find in the lobby of a lake resort. RIGHT: My client asked for the bar to be separate from the kitchen, so it would create another gathering place for guests. The mirrored wall serves up another lake view.

Your home makes memories. It's fluid and ever evolving. Embrace change.

bedroom—in its own wing of the house—may be one of my favorite moments of any I've designed, because it has the luxe aesthetic of some of the world's best spas. When you walk in, you see the blue lake sparkling outside the walls of French-paneled windows. A flickering limestone fireplace supplies a primal comfort. And, of course, a bed swaddled in mega-high thread count linens is perfect for curling up in. Along one wall, are metallic sculptures by artist Paul Villinski, who transforms aluminum soda cans he finds on the streets of New York City into fluttering butterflies.

PREVIOUS OVERLEAF LEFT: An antique apothecary chest. PREVIOUS OVERLEAF RIGHT: Barrel-back dining chairs are ultra-comfy. After nightfall, the firelight flickers in the Sputnik-inspired light fixtures, adding a dose of magic to this client's lengthy dinner parties. OPPOSITE: Details at all angles add immeasurable joy.

ABOVE: A Nepalese gown is pure art in this sitting area. OPPOSITE: Because the wall on the stairs to the basement was so large, we decided to transform it into floor-to-ceiling bookshelves with varying shapes of cubbies—a practical way to give texture. Staining it black allowed the silhouettes of this collection of white pottery to pop.

If you love to entertain, add a piece here and there that prompts others to ask questions that will get the conversation started —whether it's rare, out of place, or downright hilarious.

I wanted this powder room to feel like a gem in the crown of the entire home. We designed a gilt and hand-painted wallcovering for a bathroom without a shower or tub.

PREVIOUS OVERLEAF: In the kitchen, we clad the refrigerator to look like an armoire and stained it the same color as the great room's bar. We had the range hood custom made; the counters and backsplash are Macaubas quartzite with dynamic horizontal veining. RIGHT: The client's primary bedroom is her inner sanctuary, sheathed in a soft snakeskin-patterned wallpaper.

138

Pillows emblazoned with gray crowned cranes have a sense of humor, lending a lighthearted touch to the primary bedroom. I found the antique mirrors in North Carolina and installed them on either side behind the nightstands to capture light off the lake water and bounce it back into the room.

With its protective brass hardware edging, campaign furniture has the well-traveled appearance of an antique steamer trunk. OPPOSITE: Butterfly sculptures by Paul Villinski are made of recycled cans found on Manhattan streets.

The walls of her en suite bathroom may look like wallpaper, but they're actually brass-and-marble tiles. We thought through each and every drawer of the vanity for functionality—down to outlets for curling irons and hair dryers. Note that some of the drawer pulls were installed vertically for added interest.

opposites ATTRACT

Even when I'm working on a newly built home for clients that want to start over from scratch, I aim to make each room look like it was collected and curated over decades. And just as art and objects often need to play off one another to maximize their beauty, you want to do the same thing with your textiles and upholstery. Like a song, a room that strikes all one note would be more than monotonous. Fabrics are a great opportunity for pattern play—stripes against suzani, florals against ticking. Try to join simple and more cacophonous motifs together. When in doubt, my advice is always to attempt it; you can rethink your approach later if you're not in love with the results.

Unexpected finds are also one of my trademarks, and every year, we go on buying trips to Marrakech (for lighting and rugs) and Paris (to unearth buried treasure in the flea markets). I'm always seeking out things for clients that you can't find anywhere else on earth, like the hand-carved teak Rajasthani columns from a nineteenth-century temple I had built into the soffit of a client's home bar. Or the 1970s brass cocktail table by Jacques Duval Brasseur I found secreted away in a back warehouse in Paris—a sculptural brass praying mantis with a glowing mica tail; it imbues every happy hour with Parisian joie de vivre.

OPPOSITE: A turquoise rock is a fitting curio in the home of a gem-obsessed client. ABOVE: We bring some of the best memories of clients' lives into their homes through cherry-picked antiques that tell a story—often found through plenty of late-night deep dives on 1stDibs.

artful
LIVING

If you've never done a remodel before—like these clients, who'd built homes from scratch in the past but never revamped one of their own—the process can be nothing short of daunting. But this family had no choice. When they bought this place, it sorely needed an overhaul: it was mired in the nineties, with oddly arched windows, thick granite countertops, and moldings that had all the charm of an airport hotel.

For their new home, this family asked for a serene, textural space that wasn't too punchy with color. We began by identifying their style with magazine clippings and Pinterest, and then doing an inventory of the pieces they wanted to keep. Their art horde was truly jaw-dropping, including a lithograph of John Lennon's handwritten "Lucy in the Sky with Diamonds" and a painting of Kate Moss by Tony Scherman.

No surface went untouched. After the architect tweaked the home's bones and replaced the windows, we stained the existing floors a gray-blonde tint and sheathed practically every wall—ceilings, too!—in grass cloth wallpaper. That's one of my go-to tricks for upgrading drywall without dealing with the dust and expense of sanding it down. The cosseting effect is a little like a new cashmere sweater: luxe and comforting.

PREVIOUS OVERLEAF: In the entry, the teetering legs of a crane sculpture are echoed by the lines in an equally lanky console. RIGHT: In the dining room, we installed two handblown chandeliers—updated versions of a Sputnik chandelier that tether the line between vintage and new. When lit, they cast the whole space in dreamlike shadows. The cool tones in the blue rug offset all the taupes, while the texture and nap of the rug supply a plush, warm feel underfoot.

PAGES 152–53: Even the draperies were textural, with a leading edge in faux snakeskin. Why shouldn't everything we touch in life be a little lavish? PREVIOUS OVERLEAF: A pair of foo dogs are believed to maximize happiness and bring good fortune into your home. RIGHT: Art can change the world. In your own home, it certainly has the potential to be a mood-altering substance, lifting your spirits every time you stroll past.

CLOCKWISE FROM TOP LEFT: A horde of fresh peonies on a tea-height table. Strict vertical lines on swivel chairs play nicely with a painting depicting architectural beams. Detailed objects encourage the eye to travel a room. This side table made from a petrified slice of wood weighs nearly a ton. Cuttings from the garden. Go wild with wallpaper in a powder bath. OVERLEAF LEFT: Milo Baughman 1970s chairs dressed in their original crushed velvet add instant panache to this home office. OVERLEAF RIGHT: Lined with glass, these antique Chinese doors provide privacy and sound protection, but still allow light to flow.

ABOVE: This home is filled with various textiles and finishes, but keeping many at a similar scale provided a thread of unity throughout the spaces. OPPOSITE: Antiqued 3D mirrored tiles on the bar backsplash cast glimmer in all directions. The glass shelving illuminates at night. The lithograph is John Lennon's handwritten "Lucy in the Sky with Diamonds."

PREVIOUS OVERLEAF: An open fixture over the island allows daylight to flow. ABOVE: We wanted to keep the kitchen rich; an all-white look wouldn't have worked. Key to the look? This custom hood that we designed in brushed stainless steel, with black oiled straps and polished nickel bolts. OPPOSITE: Rare Cristallo Extreme quartzite countertops.

Be confident with pattern play. Try combining small and large prints together.

In the open living room, we turned a petrified slice of wood into a side table—it's so heavy it's nearly unliftable, but it juxtaposes against the super-soft chenille sofas perfectly. In lieu of a traditional coffee table, two leather-wrapped ottomans are sturdy enough to hold a tray of drinks and still put your feet up. Adding a dose of yellow to the bookshelves? The client's dad's old stash of *National Geographic*. Artful en masse, and super fun to flip through when the latest viral videos have lost their lustre.

One of my favorite design moments in this project is the office, complete with 1970s Milo Baughman chairs in their original crushed velvet upholstery. Because this room is right off the dining room, it had to feel private, so I installed vintage carved Chinese doors that would allow light to flow and lined them with glass as a sound barrier.

PREVIOUS OVERLEAF: An art piece painted in colored wax by Tony Scherman of his muse Kate Moss.
OPPOSITE: Using a flat paint on the primary bedroom walls gives off an almost suede-like effect.

OPPOSITE: The primary bedroom sitting area is a little retreat for these clients, with a cocoon of textures and sheathed in chocolate-hued silk wallpaper. The coffee table is higher than the sofa so you can actually put your feet up. ABOVE, CLOCKWISE FROM TOP LEFT: A bronze light fixture; embroidered linen Roman shades; hand-embroidered koi and lily pad upholstery on the armchair; a cut-velvet bolster.

ABOVE: The homeowners' serene spa bath, with a marble bench that seems to float out from the wall within the steam shower. OPPOSITE: We chose bold light fixtures throughout the home to mirror the strength of the clients' art collection.

frame the ROOM

Vincent Van Gogh knew it. Gustav Klimt, too. If you're going to create a masterpiece, you've got to frame it properly—one reason some of the most renowned artists throughout history made their own frames for many of their paintings.

Occasionally, rooms can use the same level of deference. Perhaps it's a private cocktail bar just off the kitchen. Or a dining room that has the same luxe appeal as a Michelin-starred Provençal restaurant. When I want to stop you in your tracks, I'll often have my builder install a hand-carved arched doorway right into the drywall—often one that was salvaged from a long-ago, torn-down ancient structure in India or Thailand. It serves as a moment of eye candy in the home's architecture and is something your guests will never expect.

If you already have stunning woodwork you want to draw eyes to, think about refinishing it—either to show off its natural grain or to keep an emphasis on its graceful lines by painting part of it, like we did in the historic home at left. Just another way to make an entrance.

ABOVE: In this historical home, painting only the exterior of the moldings of this archway a crisp white emphasized its exquisite detailing while lightening it for the modern era. OPPOSITE: Delicately scalloped edges on an antique carved doorway from India transform this dining room into a portal to another world.

get
PERSONAL

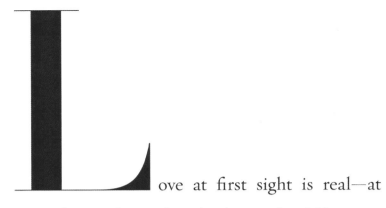

Love at first sight is real—at least when it comes to houses. I knew with one glance that this home should become mine. There was just one problem: it wasn't for sale. Still, the place made my heart sing. It was just the sort of MidMod house you would see on Mulholland Drive in the paradisiacal Hollywood Hills. So, I did the thing you're never supposed to do in today's strained real estate market: I went up to the door and knocked. The lady who answered—a former Miss Colorado, then in her eighties—couldn't have been nicer, and gave me tea and a private tour when I told her I loved her home and wanted to buy it. I even sent a note a few months later begging to purchase the property. A year and half after that, she decided to move to Arizona and told me it was ours.

I remember distinctly saying, "I'm not going to remodel." She'd kept her home absolutely pristine, with wall-to-wall white carpet. Not ideal for young kids! Not long after we moved in, my kids made a blueberry smoothie in the kitchen—and the carpet had to be taken out and replaced with stained wood floors. We covered most of the drywall and ceilings in grass cloth for a cozy texture and revamped the other spaces over time.

PREVIOUS OVERLEAF: Our sweet Labrador James admiring our pair of Asian elmwood chairs.
OPPOSITE: For my family's own home, a warm welcome was a must. I had a pair of midcentury snake candleholder sconces from India wired for lighting and love the glow they cast against the chinoiserie wallcovering (framed here like an art piece).

Everyone says, "Let your home tell your story." That means, "Display what speaks to you."

Feng shui is important to me, so we very quickly painted our double front door a juicy raspberry red (a symbol of luck and encouraging energy at the gateway to your home, especially if your facade faces south or west). When you walk in, you look straight out to a large bank of windows, and beyond that, our gardens and pool. Ninety-nine percent of the time, our drapery remains open to the outside so the abundant daylight can pour in.

One of our most prescient changes was taking out the upstairs laundry room to create a working kitchen that would sit behind our main cook space. Since it was a small room, I could go a little crazy; I opted to lacquer it all a rich blue, using door handles I found in Asia and transformed into cabinet pulls to make it all look like furniture. I hate it when appliances sit out on countertops, and by making this

PREVIOUS OVERLEAF: In our formal living room, I had a custom mobile made to hang instead of a light fixture. I love the way it moves in a breeze and twinkles in the sun. OPPOSITE: Collectibles we've found over the years bring joy to a corner of our living room. OVERLEAF: The coffee table is an antique Asian bed I had modified for height. OVERLEAF RIGHT: Clerestory windows allow light to flow.

Let your home be a reflection of the largest life you can live.

entirely separate kitchen, we could keep our showpiece kitchen, with its hand-painted wallcoverings and Calacatta marble countertops, truly immaculate—and, frankly, that is not a word you can often use in a house with kids!

Throughout my family's home, collections and *objets* tell the story of our lives and loves. Hung between soft linen drapery in the living room is an oil-on-canvas abstract painted by my grandmother in the 1950s. The delicate clay horse statue, gifted to me by my mother, is a loved keepsake. There's even a Lucite-based dining table the home's previous owner gifted us. I think she knew that it belonged here, in this house, just like us.

PREVIOUS OVERLEAF: We love to gather in this conversation area by the fire. OPPOSITE: Pieces by my grandmother, who was born in Austria in 1907 and attended the Academy of Fine Arts Vienna. She later taught art at Princeton University, and I would visit her every summer and sit enraptured in her studio as she showed me how to block print and press botanicals that we'd pick in her gardens.

ABOVE: Next to our main kitchen, I designed a working cook space in a rich blue, where we could tuck our countertop appliances out of sight. (You'd never know it, but the door on the right is secretly a broom closet.) OPPOSITE: Lattice bamboo chairs bring a barefoot, Caribbean vibe to our breakfast nook—an ode to my mother, who grew up in St. Thomas in the U.S. Virgin Islands.

PREVIOUS OVERLEAF: Campaign drawer pulls, Calacatta marble, and hand-painted wallcovering have made this kitchen one of my many happy places. RIGHT, CLOCKWISE FROM TOP LEFT: Black lampshades are effortlessly cool. This Lucite dining table was a gift from the previous owner, a former Miss Colorado. Snake candleholders I had wired for our foyer. Collected pottery, travel trinkets, and a hand-painted mural wallcovering make our main kitchen both fun and functional. My all-time favorite furniture designer Jacques Duval Brasseur′s beloved praying mantis cocktail table, unearthed at a Paris flea market. Our conversation-starting sitting area, set for tea.

196

OPPOSITE: A piece by Thomas McKnight gives our sitting room a lake view. ABOVE: Adorning our bar: a stash of *ibeji* sculptures from Nigeria, where I lived as a child. The glass display box holds a baby bottle that has coral growing on it—a constant reminder not to litter our oceans.

ABOVE: My personal home office. OPPOSITE: A self-portrait of my grandmother hangs over an antique Victorian sofa, which I had painted a fiery orange and reupholstered in cut velvet. The table is from a trip to Egypt. I brought the brass lamp in the background home from a trip to Morocco. OVERLEAF: I repurposed the hand-painted screen I made for the Beverly Hills Greystone Mansion Design Showcase house to be used as a fanciful headboard.

storytelling SECRETS

Just like a person, a room can be devoid of personality. It can talk a lot but have nothing to say. That's why each space I design is tailored specifically to the clients who live there, so that if you were to stroll in and stay a spell, you'd be able to learn something about them without their uttering a word.

No home should ever look like a showroom, so every home I design tells a story. When we first begin working together, I'll often ask clients about their most cherished memories. For a couple who were married in Bali, we made a hand-carved wooden sculpture of an Indonesian goddess and placed it center stage on their entry console, where it conjures romantic recollections with each passing glance. If your ancestor's circa 1925 Lachenal vase holds special significance for you, we may pull colors from it to inform your backsplash tile or the wallcovering in your powder room. Of course, sometimes creating a personal home is less about your belongings and more about how you feel and look in the space. Perhaps you have olive-green eyes. We'll be sure to dress your house so they always pop—with complementary hues.

Teasing out memories from the clients can lead to design ideas that add instant charm to any residential project. Better yet, it means that once the project is done, it's practically guaranteed to be instantly welcoming to them. They may have never even lived there, but the moment they walk through the doors, it feels like home.

ABOVE: Sometimes personalization is as simple as opting for a regal muse portrait in your home office.
OPPOSITE: If you have an obsession with cumulus clouds—how they change throughout the day, like movable sculptures in the sky—hunt down a photograph that captures the feeling of that for your study.

ONE ROOM
at a time

Life is colorful, so why limit your palette to bland hues? Give yourself permission to go for it! Every single room in your home can be a star; you don't need certain spaces to slink off onto the sidelines as supporting cast. For proof, look no further than the rooms in this chapter, some of which I designed for showhouses (pro bono projects to benefit a charity). The first is a ladies' lounge I decorated at the fifty-five-room Greystone Mansion, that's secreted away on a manicured garden in Beverly Hills.

When you give me carte blanche, I push the envelope as far as I can. For this space, where women would swan in between dinner courses to powder their noses and refresh their lipstick, I chose an Hermès-orange wallpaper to create an envelope that would stop you in your tracks. Pink would have been too obvious for a women's room, and this hue is still feminine while serving to give your skin a bit of a glow. (Ever pragmatic, I put some of it on a folding screen, which I hauled home and turned into a headboard.) Preventing the room from reading as too sweet: an cool painting by figurative artist Alex Katz, sleek Lucite tables for freshening your makeup, and custom armchairs I designed in a decidedly masculine silhouette.

PREVIOUS OVERLEAF: At a show house in the Beverly Hills Greystone Mansion, we created the ultimate ladies' lounge. OPPOSITE AND OVERLEAF: Hand-painted orange wallpaper is a scene stealer in this thoroughly cinematic property. Note the Lucite vanity tables, portrait by artist Alex Katz, and custom armchairs I had upholstered in luxe cut velvet.

Chandeliers are like diamond earrings for your home. Dimmers can control the mood.

The second room, in *House Beautiful*'s Whole Home concept house, exemplifies my firmly held belief that every dining room should be dual-purpose. We married this one with a study, exalting a collection of library books as a graphic touch in built-in shelves roosting in the upper ceiling alongside wallpaper from my Liesl Collection, inspired by my grandmother's own painting. Of course, there is a bar—in case you need a dram of Scotch while poring over your Proust. Over the table, we hung artichoke-shaped lighting fixtures (on dimmers) that infuse a warm, romantic luminescence, almost like candlelight, into the space.

The last spaces here are close to home, literally—our very own design studio. We worked hard to adorn the interiors, in part so that clients could stroll in and get an instant feel for the quality of our work, but also so our team could live our best lives at the office. Dull, monotonous interiors inspire no one, least of all a design firm that buzzes with creative types day and night. It's just as fun as it looks. Don't believe me? Come by and see for yourself.

We brought the ceilings in this *House Beautiful* magazine project down to earth just a bit by hanging twelve artichoke-inspired chandeliers with a total of 1,400 gilt and white petals. The wallpaper on the upper walls is based on work by my artist grandmother. OVERLEAF: One of my favorite paintings by my grandmother, on loan from my collection.

This space in our Denver HQ epitomizes what our firm is known for: mixing antiques culled from my travels around the world, showstopping art and light fixtures, and clean upholstered furniture to balance it all out. The walls here are hand-painted based on a piece by my grandmother. I found that chandelier in the Paris flea market, and its overscaled heft is perfect here.

ABOVE: One of my signature moves is to transform an antique chest into a bathroom vanity, as we did in our office powder room. The pink wallpaper here is actually made of wood veneer. OPPOSITE: Our staff kitchen, with all the comforts—and colors—of home, down to a raspberry grass cloth–covered ceiling.

the FIFTH WALL

Imagine stepping into the Sistine Chapel, looking skyward, and seeing . . . a bland, whitewashed ceiling. Or finding the celestial vaulted mural in Manhattan's Grand Central Terminal replaced with a smattering of those fiberglass office ceiling tiles. Depressing, right? That's why I always address what designers call "the fifth wall" as unforgettably as I can.

It doesn't need to be Michelangelo-worthy, but decking out your ceiling can bring untold joy to a room. You could hang graphic wallpaper—like a latticed bamboo motif in a cheeky coral color—to add instant energy overhead. Or paint riotous stripes in haphazard lines, a move that can serve to make a low ceiling feel sky-high, thanks to all the surplus verve. You could even have your contractor install open beams for a coffered appearance or ceiling medallions for a storied look that seems like it has stood the test of time for centuries. Or easily transform a powder room or guest quarters into a jewel box simply by painting the ceiling and trim a high-gloss version of the wall color. Whatever you do, don't forget to look up: the fifth wall is a finishing touch that can take your interiors to dizzying heights.

ABOVE: A black-and-white graphic pattern on the ceiling prevents the light fixture in this bedroom from reading as too ethereal. OPPOSITE: Only the legendary Lyford Trellis wallpaper could balance the visual eye candy of Dorothy Draper's 1960s barrel-backed lounge chairs.

ACKNOWLEDGMENTS

Like designing a beautiful home, it takes many hands to bring a book to life.

I must start by thanking my incredible mom and dad. You believed in me and gave me my love of traveling from the very start. That first passport you got me was also a passport to seeing the vast beauty in life, and I will be forever grateful. I also owe a debt of gratitude to my grandmother, artist Elizabeth Monath, for my greatest inheritance: all those formative hours absorbing art and design together. You were a fearless woman, and I miss you every day. All my family, Jesse, Nissa, and all my amazing friends—too many to list here: you mean so much to me, and I couldn't have done this without you.

Every designer knows that clients are the reason we get to do the dreamy work we do, and I'm exceptionally thankful for those who have become lifelong friends.

An enormous thank-you to my work family at Andrea Schumacher Interiors; I couldn't have asked for a better, more fun and dedicated team. You're absolutely brilliant.

Thanks also to all the companies that bring our design vision to life, including my go-tos—Kravet, Visual Comfort, and Vanguard.

Special thanks to the truly top-notch team behind this book: photographers Roger Davies, William Abranowicz, Emily Minton Redfield, Durston Saylor, and Laure Joliet; agent Jill Cohen; writer Kathryn O'Shea-Evans; publisher Gibbs Smith and editor Madge Baird; designer Doug Turshen and compositor David Huang; stylists Steven Pappas, Eleanor Roper, Tawney Waldo, Natalie Warady, and my creative director, Troy Rivington.

And, of course, appreciation to all the wonderful hotels around the world where I stay, for endless inspiration. El Fenn Marrakech, you're my favorite.

First Edition
26 25 24 23 22   5 4 3 2 1

Text © 2022 Andrea Monath Schumacher

End sheet and case art by Elizabeth Monath, © Andrea
Monath Schumacher

Photographs © 2022 as follows:
William Abranowicz, 11–37, 75–115
Roger Davies, 8, 41–71, 118–145, 149–175, 178–203, 223
Vivian Johnson, 38
Laure Joliet, 207–211
Dustin Peck, 221
Emily Minton Redfield, 39, 72, 73, 116, 117, 146, 147,
176, 177, 204, 205, 213–219
Durston Saylor, 220

Published by
Gibbs Smith
P.O. Box 667
Layton, Utah 84041
1.800.835.4993 orders
www.gibbs-smith.com

Designed by Doug Turshen with David Huang
Printed and bound in China

Gibbs Smith books are printed on either recycled, 100%
post-consumer waste, FSC-certified papers or on paper
produced from sustainable PEFC-certified forest/
controlled wood source. Learn more at www.pefc.org.

Library of Congress Control Number: 2021947700

ISBN: 978-1-4236-6016-3